Axe, Fire, Mule

The Ozarks

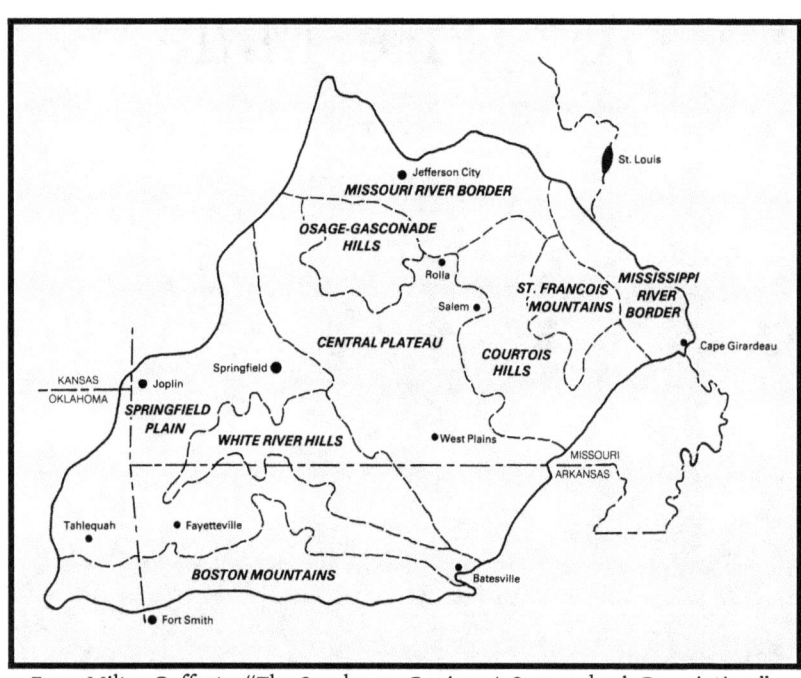

From Milton Rafferty, "The Ozarks as a Region: A Geographer's Description." *OzarksWatch*, SMSU Center for Ozarks Studies, vol. 1, no. 4, 1988, p.3.

Axe, Fire, Mule

Poems by

C. D. Albin

Golden Antelope Press
715 E. McPherson
Kirksville, Missouri 63501
2018

Copyright ©2018 by C. D. Albin

Cover Image Copyright ©2018 by Dawn Surratt

Interior Photographs ©2018 by Kelli Jean Albin

National Council of Teachers of English holds the copyrights for the five poems previously published in *Teaching English in the Two-Year College*: "Downsized"; "English as a Second Language"; "Following Mr. Parks"; "Sign"; and "Speech Lessons." Used with permission.

All rights reserved. No portion of this publication may be duplicated in any way without the expressed written consent of the publisher, except in the form of brief excerpts or quotations for review purposes.

ISBN: 978-1-936135-54-7 (1-936135-54-X)

Library of Congress Control Number: 2018937926

Published by:
Golden Antelope Press
715 E. McPherson
Kirksville, Missouri 63501

Available at:
Golden Antelope Press
715 E. McPherson
Kirksville, Missouri, 63501
Phone: (660) 665-0273
http://www.goldenantelope.com
Email: ndelmoni@gmail.com

To Mary Maxine Albin,
my mother,
my exemplar for grace and courage,
faith and resilience.

Contents

Acknowledgements — v

Ozark Dark — 1
Ozark Dark 2
Here and Now 3
All Else 4
Radney's Tree 6
Speck of Shine 8
Searcher 9
Lament 10
Parade 11
The Runner 12
Stick Pony 13
Irish Wilderness 14

Marooned — 15
Thrown 16
I Will Send Her Safely Past 17
Shadow Box 18
Sinkhole 19
Blessed Those Days 20
White as Lime 21
Allen's Boy 23
Nine Days 24
Glaucoma 25
Hard of Hearing 26
Marooned 28

Axe, Fire, Mule — 29

- Barn Chore — 30
- This Same Field — 31
- Intruder — 32
- What Drought Has Brought — 33
- Burn Ban — 34
- Pharaoh Dreamed of Cattle — 35
- This Side — 37
- Mine — 38
- Restoration — 40
- White-tail — 42
- Axe, Fire, Mule — 43

Rose of Sharon — 45

- Rose of Sharon — 46
- Downsized — 47
- English as a Second Language — 48
- Speech Lessons — 49
- Sign — 50
- Following Mr. Parks — 51
- Endgame — 52
- Revision — 54
- At Shiloh — 55
- Soldier Home — 56
- Old Order — 57

Will and Testament — 59

- Cicero Jack, Farmer, Rues the Ruin of an Ozark River — 60
- Cicero Jack Considers the Cougar's Return — 62
- Cicero Jack Contemplates the Heart-Stays People — 64
- Cicero Jack Ponders Relics of the Osage — 65
- Cicero Jack and Snake at Sunset — 66
- Cicero Jack Remembers Tom Cochran's Boy — 68
- The Late Love Song of Cicero Jack — 70
- The Will and Testament of Cicero Jack — 71

The Author — 75

Acknowledgements:

- *ALIVE Magazine*: "Cicero Jack Ponders Relics of the Osage"
- *Big Muddy*: "Blessed Those Days"; "Marooned"; "White-tail"; "Cicero Jack Remembers Tom Cochran's Boy"
- *Cantos*: "Shadow Box"; "The Late Love Song of Cicero Jack"; "Hard of Hearing"; "Restoration"; "The Irish Wilderness"
- *The Cape Rock*: "Barn Chore"; "Cicero Jack Considers the Cougar's Return"; "The Will and Testament of Cicero Jack"; "Glaucoma"; "This Side"
- *Cave Region Review*: "Burn Ban"; "Here and Now"; "Ozark Dark"; "Pharaoh Dreamed of Cattle"; "Searcher"; "White as Lime"
- *The Chaffin Journal*: "Soldier Home"
- *CrossRoads: A Journal of Southern Culture*: "Lament" (as "Ozark Lament")
- *Crosstimbers: A Multicultural Interdisciplinary Journal*: "Rose of Sharon"
- *Concho River Review*: "Axe, Fire, Mule"
- *Flint Hills Review*: "Radney's Tree"
- *Front Range Review*: "Allen's Boy"
- *Kentucky English Bulletin*: "At Shiloh"
- *The Heartland Review*: "All Else" (as "Neighborhood Watch"); "Stick Pony"
- *LiturgicalCredo*: "Old Order" (as "Plain People")
- *Mid-America Poetry Review*: "Intruder"; "This Same Field"
- *The Mochila Review*: "I'll Send Her Safely Past"
- *Moon City Review*: "Cicero Jack Contemplates the Heart-Stays People"; "Cicero Jack, Farmer, Rues the Ruin of an Ozark River"; "Endgame"
- *The Pikeville Review*: "Parade"; "Sinkhole"; "What Drought Has Brought"
- *Red Rock Review*: "Nine Days" (as "Belief")
- *Rockhurst Review*: "The Runner"
- *San Pedro River Review*: "Thrown"
- *SLANT: A Journal of Poetry*: "Cicero Jack and Snake at Sunset"; "Revision"
- *Storm Country*: "Mine"
- *Teaching English in the Two-Year College*: "Downsized"; "English as a Second Language"; "Following Mr. Parks"; "Sign"; "Speech Lessons"

Rise, plead your case
before the mountains,
and let the hills
hear your voice.

Micah 6:1

Ozark Dark

Ozark Dark

Most nights I wake to cacophonies
of coyotes in the near pasture,
high pitched yips following a frenzy

of kill-lust, bellies filled with rabbits,
mice, maybe a luckless barn cat—then
silence sudden as a snake strike. Soon

come bedeviled bays from our Bluetick
ranging in caged torment along the
fenced ridgetop, his howls drifting heartsick

over the hollows. Weary, I shift
weight to stare out the window, ponder
lamentations of the Ozark dark.

Here and Now

> Man brings all things to the test of himself,
> and this is notably true of lightning.
> —Aldo Leopold

Sawdust scrim settles as he
sinks the chainsaw deep within

a fallen trunk, makes quick work
of an oak even lightning

took a year to kill. Last spring,
when night bolts lit the hollow,

a jolt of sound pounded his
ear drums, bounced him to his feet

beside the bed and left him
wandering in full dark, his

own house a mazy box built
by strangers. No Leopold

counting rings, he looks ahead
to months of dry oak burning

in his stove, bullying winds
bluffing beneath the eaves. His creed—

let pretend farmers ponder
past as prologue. He serves here

and now, does what needs doing
to keep lights on, his house warm.

All Else

No matter the new conservation
officer's patient pleas, carcasses

of coyotes still drape fence posts down
these country roads, gray bodies hanging

headless to warn mates who, stalking lamb
or calf, may steal food from family

plates. I count four dead per quarter mile,
consider the hunter's squinted eye,

its necessary gift for seeing
a world in the width of a cross hair.

My own eye roams rocky pastures rimmed
in cedar, oak, hickory—a green

wall hemming the dens of fox, bobcat,
all else that instinct prompts to watch, wait.

Radney's Tree

    Old Boze reaches back to the
    thread-thin beginning of his

    own memory, recalling
    borrowed hearsay received from

    men long gone. *Radney was a*
    horse thief, he says, waving his

    blunt hand at a green mass of
    eastern ridge. *They chased him through*

    awful country, all rocky
    hollows and dried-up creek beds,

    till he stopped beneath the tree
    they hung him from. We squint off

    to the east, as if we can
    spot the limb, the rope, even

    the dangling man in that great
    wall of forest. Grandaddy

    had a hand in that, Boze says,
    bringing us back. My uncles

    chuckle, give in to quick grins
    before lips tighten, go thin.

Speck of Shine

Run a gun-and-pawn like the
Pair-a-Dice and you'll see most
anything. This morning came

a woman with her daughter,
neither bigger than a whip.
The daughter's face was framed by

bird's nest hair her mama swept
behind one ear, revealing
a speck of shine in the lobe.

Pure gold, she swore. *What'll
you give?* The girl cupped her ear,
hissed about a boy, a gift,

but the mother slapped away
the protecting hand. *Your sign
says cash for gold. How much this?*

I thought to close, claim sickness,
but the girl cursed, set the stud
on the counter and banged out

the door. Her mother stepped near.
You've got a slick price in mind.
I slid five ones near her reach,

stared at the place where she snatched
the bills. Then I worked a cloth
back and forth across that spot.

Searcher

When they asked him why he failed
to come in with the others,
but stayed out all that moonless
night groping his way along

the hollow's rocky slopes, back
and forth across its snaky
floor while his flashlight faded,
he would only say *the child,*

the lonely lost child, making
believe he meant the straw-haired
toddler he finally found
curled with her collie asleep

at the base of an oak, and
not the bloodied, belt-bruised boy
he still is, who haunted the
same hollow and never told.

Lament

I am the son who found him.
Later, when they asked, I said
it was a thing he preferred,
to die alone in dark night,
clutching only a weathered
cedar post he had driven
himself. What I didn't say
was how surprised I was—not
at him or death, but myself,
that out of all I could have
hated, I despised most that
swayed, half-rotten corner post,
for being what he reached for.

Parade

From a barber's chair I stare
at him, an old man pinching
a menthol he can barely
lift to his lips, clawbone hands
trembling as he gasps for air.
His whispery voice conjures
words inside my ear: *They'll take
that parade right down this street,
won't they?* I'm clueless who he's
asking. Me or the barber?
But he goes on: *Ain't this the
way they'll take?* Joe rests scissors
on my shoulder, tells him the
old soldiers march tomorrow.
After a breathy pause we
learn he fought across France, brought
home a bullet near his spine.
Still there, he says. *Couldn't march
in no parade anyway.*

The Runner

At the crest of the clay hill
he flinches, ducking toward the

ditch as the vulture spreads wide
wings and lifts, lurching aloft,

leaving behind a mashed hound,
hindquarters crushed, eye socket

a clean bowl into which the
sun pours. Weak-kneed, the runner

stumbles through ditch weeds, counting
heartbeats until he can take

the road again, striving to
forget what running is for.

Stick Pony

Though bays grazed in the corral
near the house, I thinned boot soles
galloping behind that mount's
ebony head, its airy
body wispy as wind till
rough play parted the stitched seam
and gray batting bulged from the
cleaved crown. Stored forgotten in
a closet, wound dust-coated
for decades, that pony loomed
to mind today outside a
funeral home, its iron
cousin a hitching post—black
horse head facing west. Tracing
the blind gaze to rows of scribed
stones in the distance, I saw
once again that familiar
bobbing head fill the foreground,
felt the jarring of boot heels
gouging soft loam. Astounding
how firmly memory held
that pounding pace, as if I
had been riding a lifetime.

Irish Wilderness

> *A wilderness ... is hereby recognized*
> *as an area where the earth and its*
> *community of life are untrammeled*
> *by man, where man himself*
> *is a visitor who does not remain.*
> —The Wilderness Act of 1964

They wed a priest's dream to their own and so
purchased parcels of Missouri's wild land
along the Eleven Point because they

could afford no better. Now we burnish
tales of their vanishing into legend,
gaze upon the great second growth forest

that remains, and shiver for newcomers
who dare enter, nodding to each other
when they lose their way and must be rescued

by locals on mountain ponies. We fail
to remember how our lank ancestors
cleared the first forest in a violence

of axes that echoed the war years when
bushwhackers lived to loot and burn, their paths
swaths of fire that sent entire towns into

exile, Irish pioneers suddenly
remade into refugees fleeing charred
homesteads and war-wild hearts of their neighbors.[1]

---

[1] Editor's Preface, *On the Mission in Missouri & Fifty Years Ago: A Memoir*, Crystal Payton: "The Irish Wilderness is land and legend. The land is a 16,500 acre wilderness preserve in the Missouri Ozarks, between the Eleven Point and Current rivers. The legend is of a lost colony of pre-Civil War Irish immigrant families who came to settle the land under the direction and encouragement of a young Irish priest, John Joseph Hogan."

Marooned

Thrown

Onscreen, a kid from Lubbock
lasts the full eight on a big
bay, but I root for those who
land in the dust, their failures

recalling my first rides on
my uncle's back, an oval
rug our arena as he
spun on all fours, threatening

to throw me while I clung like
a bug. Tennis shoes for spurs,
I tumbled to the rug bunched
in small hillocks like hoof-pawed

dirt. Those soft, cushioned landings
gave me no warning of the
fat pony that would pin my
leg against a fence post, or

the anger that flared in my
uncle's voice when I couldn't
rein her away, his rough hands
yanking the headstall, pounding

her neck until she bucked me
onto the railing where I
hung, face down and bawling, thrown
rider above blood-red clay.

I Will Send Her Safely Past

Mother calls us back inside,
screen door slapping clapboard where
she's thrown it wide, her right arm
waving us through the kitchen
to the picture window's view

of greening woods. There she yells,
and we spot the spring-thin bear—
black, ambling on outsized paws
clumsy as teenagers' feet.
The hound pup howls, gives chase while

my sister gasps, hands drumming
thick windowpane. Pup at heel,
the bear lurches into woods.
Hours later Mother approves
the backyard swing, my sister

claiming the seat. Pushing, I
send her out, up, ponytail
flicking while her ground shadow
lengthens, shrinks, lengthens again.
I push harder but the shape

transforms, becomes a creature
rising on hind legs. I push
again, determined to send
her past that shadow, until
she breaks my trance with her cries.

Shadow Box

He brought home no war stories
from New Guinea, only his
uniform and small items

now mounted on velvet in
the shadow box—dog tags and
souvenir bullet, service

medal and marksman's badge. A
sparse collection, so after
he passed we added the flag,

tightly folded, the fading
photo of him still stateside—
thin, boyish in uniform,

spectacled. We grandchildren
knew only the older man,
the jaunty gait and soft laugh,

face a bit like Astaire's, so
we never thought to ask what
kind of war he had, or what

dreams so often woke him to
sweat-drenched bed linens inside
a clapboard house of shadows.

Sinkhole

The ground opens in the night.
Come morning, my stern uncle
sums his herd like a teacher
counting heads. We clear balky

cattle from the field, chance close
to the crater's edge. *Likely
there's a cave beneath,* he says.
Land falls when the roof gives way.

I watch him point a palsied
hand, follow its uncertain
line to where he thinks failure
of earth began. A cedar's

tip shows green as new growth near
the clayed center of the bowl.
I inch close and clench my eyes,
feel the falling of my bones.

Blessed Those Days

In boyhood I bought baseball cards
and bubble gum at Preacher Roe's,[2]
blessed those days Preacher himself

manned the counter, passing me
penny change with the same left hand
that snapped curves, fastballs,

even banned spitters for St. Louis
and far off Brooklyn. Outside,
as cars spun down a boulevard

named for Porter Wagoner, I opened
packs of cards hoping for heroes
like Lou Brock, Hank Aaron,

Roberto Clemente, never knowing
how often Preacher's left hand had
slapped the back of a man named Jackie.

---

[2] Elwyn Charles "Preacher" Roe was a Major League baseball player who pitched for the Cardinals, Pirates, and Dodgers. A native of Ash Flat, Arkansas, Roe resided for most of his life in West Plains, Missouri, where he owned and operated Preacher Roe's Supermarket. Roger Kahn devoted a chapter of his classic book *The Boys of Summer* to Roe.

White as Lime

    Red slow-walked me through that first
    summer job, taught me to chalk

    baseline and batter's box, drag
    an infield smooth and rake the

    mound for each night's Little League
    game. But tending infields chafed

    him, rubbed him raw like tines that
    bit sun-baked clay at our feet—

    till that heat-thick morning in
    July when he didn't show,

    and the city's mowers choked
    on lime poured into their tanks.

    Our squatty boss summoned me
    to his office behind the

    bleachers, half-moons of cloth dark
    beneath his arms. *Red's done it*

    this time. Best say what you know.
    I held tongue, pondered why Red

    would chance a trick like this when
    outfield grass needed cutting

    and *Play ball!* never yielded
    to anything but rain. Noon

    saw a patrol car roll in,
    park where we'd clotted along

    the first base line. A stout cop
    hauled Red out, swatted his head

for calling *Hey boys!* and marched
him to the office. I prayed

he'd swallow enough pride that
his troubles would soften, though

he soon strutted back, the cop
scowling at his side. Near the

car he caught my eye. I heard
Rake 'em smooth, Chief, watched him point

a bony finger at my
chest. Then he forced a twitchy

grin, his stubble-growth of beard
now coarse, patchy, white as lime.

Allen's Boy

He's not built like his father,
more linebacker or catcher
than the lean point guard Allen
was roaming this country court
from end to end, tough shots made
with lazy flicks of the wrist
I envied but couldn't stop
through countless matches, Allen
always the man. Now there is
only this burly boy, ten,
huffing as he launches shots
from his shoulder that bang the
backboard like field stones against
a barn. He inherited
no shooter's touch, no lithe vault
into air, only enough
second-hand daddy tales that
he must ask again whether
his father really ran this
court, or really gazed on these
encircling trees. Spinning the
ball, searching for small comfort
of fingertips on a seam,
I wait till the heft feels right
before lofting a jumper
that barely reaches the rim.
Yes, I say, *he ran here, lungs
burning until he gulped air
the way you are now—the way
you will tomorrow. You are
here,* I tell him. *You are real.*

Nine Days

Nine days have passed since I raised
my toddler son high enough
to peer into my father's
coffin, and still he chants a
child's charm, *Not Papa.* Hearing
him, Linda curses my faith
that our son could gaze on that
waxy mask and recognize
anything familiar. *What
were you thinking,* she asks, but
I turn away, unwilling
to admit it was less thought
than fleshly need, mere longing
to fill bare hands with the soft,
wriggling weight of my son, who
told me then and tells me now
what we each need to believe.

Glaucoma

Field test, the nurse calls this tiresome task,
me clicking away at pin dots of light
that blip on the screen, or straining to spot

faint afterglows, my thumb a jumpy
trigger finger. *Stay with me,* she urges,
concerned that I catch every burst

of fool's gold passing through my
field of vision, but I need no test
to see the field is shrinking, darkness

closing in. When I was nine the night
would fall like that, sneaking from all sides
until the hay field where I played

was scarcely wider than my reach,
fireflies lighting moments narrower
than breath, but never the way home.

Hard of Hearing

    As children, we giggled jokes
    about the near deaf, aunts and
    uncles from my father's side

    who shouted *Louder! Speak up!*
    during every discussion.
    At family gatherings

    we concocted contests meant
    to prove which cousin could cause
    the most frustration. Pitching

    our voices low, we mumbled
    into cupped hands, then raced toward
    our favorite hiding place

    beneath lacy willow limbs
    near the back porch, recounting
    our cruelties with manic zest.

    For me, already pronounced
    deaf in one ear, our jokes seemed
    harmless, the humming world as

    loud as ever. I'd never
    known a need to strain after
    words that vanished like fleet birds

    secreting in leafy woods,
    my one good ear preserving
    sound, my conscience unassailed.

    Years later, when visiting
    my dying Aunt Blanche in her
    hospital room the day I

    left for college, I struggled
    to make myself heard, to say
    I would be thinking of her

along the road, and after—
words that never reached her ear.
She lay marooned in silence,

although her own voice—soft, sharp—
lingered like a chirping bird's.
Let me hear from you, she said,

her smile stretching delicate
cheekbones, and I left, fleeing
the echoes of my own steps.

Marooned

Only men made ice cream those
summer nights when uncles, aunts,
cousins came together at

the home place on Cherry Street.
Men hunched over buckets that
rattled with rock salt and ice

cubes, took turns churning in their
Sunday shirts till starched cotton
melted flat against broad backs

and sweetness swirled in buckets
between stout legs. We children
chased each other around the

house, into the street, burning
energy at ending day
till bowls flavored with peaches,

strawberries, sometimes even
chocolate renewed our strength,
sent us laughing, calling in

the shadowed night while work-worn
men leaned marooned on porch steps,
sifting fragrant voice from voice.

Axe, Fire, Mule

Barn Chore

That first time when I was nine
I didn't lift new bales, just

dragged old ones into neater
rows along the loft floor, rolled

a few more with my shoulder,
until Uncle Joe called me

down to splash my sweaty head,
dash my face with water. I

see now how he kept careful
watch on more than chores, though a

low voice and bony stare made
him seem more warden than kin.

Finish up there, he asked, and
before I could think yes or

no he flattened a hand on
my back, sent me trotting for

the door. Outside I gulped fresh
air and savored open sky,

but I turned too soon, caught him
halfway up the ladder. Mad,

I thought he was checking the
job I'd done—until he looped

both wrists on the rung above
his head, hung in high shadow

and coughed so long I ran back,
my hands helpless as he fell.

This Same Field

    I liked to call them cairns, though
none marked a fallen soldier.
I made half those piles myself,
hefted stones the better part
of several summers, cursed
beneath my breath. My uncle
thought such work would clear my head,
move my young notions nearer
his. Yet all that time trundling
rocks to far corners of our
land, I hoped hard for other
fields. Now I'm the age he was
then, and life has circled back
to this same field of stones like
the bending of a year, a
course that ends where it begins,
here on land his will made mine.

Intruder

Sunday morning, hiking old
trails behind the house, I catch
something at the farthest edge

of vision, and turning, find
the owl already turned—head
swiveled on drought-brown body,

its claw-perch a corner post.
You, I think, and remember
porch evenings, flinch of my

own flesh at the screech, the rip
in the airy cloth of night,
though no night is here, only

blank, silent distance between
its eye and mine, until I
lean an inch too far, dislodge

a stone and startle eons
of instinct that spur the bird
to heavy, shadow-stalked flight.

What Drought Has Brought

My neighbor laughs, insists he's
country too, from that lower
belt of Illinois where loam
is moist and corn thrusts high

as Lincoln's head. But he's too
newly moved, can't feel what drought
has brought to Ozark farms where
hill men watch a glinty sky,

dread the early sere of fields.
He sees I need a sharp pick
to break his ground, stretch new fence
along his line. He wonders

if the wage is low. I shrug
as though he's fair, swing hard and
hear the flinted ring of rock.
By nine he rushes to town,

another sort of work, while
I wrestle clay and stone to
set his corner post. I take
sweet time, make my wages right.

Burn Ban

    Julie fumes as flames flick high
    from brush piles that dot old Paul's
    ridge. I count three fires and dare
    a defense: he's worked his way
    for fifty years, never lit

    the county yet. Wroth, she stomps
    bare feet on hardwood, slams our
    bedroom door. Outside I catch
    whiffs of smoke, recall I told
    him yesterday about the

    ban, bounced up his road to warn
    that word was on radio,
    TV, the woods nothing but
    tinder till we get rain. He
    waved me away, walked off through

    dust my tires had churned. Now I
    play night guard and strain to spot
    wayward sparks, my home hostage
    to whim of wind. For Julie
    all we own is a pauper's

    fortune weighed against one old
    man's pride, but I can't deny
    he so loathes to follow rules
    he might choose conflagration
    over final compromise.

Pharaoh Dreamed of Cattle

Rucked acres ripple south toward
Arkansas, Herefords dotting

dry pastures grazed to stubble
that crunches under hooves. We've

been months with no rain, high sky
unbroken except for sun

and buzzards day after day.
Pharaoh dreamed of fat cattle

rising from the river Nile
to feast on green grass, until

others came, thin-flanked ones like
mine, so hungry they ate those

ready for market, startling
Pharaoh from his sleep. These steamed

nights, sweating through sheets, I think
I would welcome some seer

from another land, Joseph
able to cull my fevered

dreams, pronounce the yea or nay
of seasons. Instead I hear

the reedy drone of insects
beyond the window, or the

sudden yips of coyotes
as they surround some lone thing

caught apart from its nest, hole,
hidden den. Come morning, I

often find small bones flashing
white in the sun. With boot toe

I sift them, play at reading
bone for sign, until bawling

cattle send me to the barn
where I load leavings of last

summer's hay, dry wind drifting
straw across dirt like tinder.

This Side

You would think he was buzzing
the house, the sound seems that close.
It drowns out the TV, makes
us duck when we run to the
window. The chopper beats west
and we spill onto the porch,
spot him above the far ridge
at the end of our forty.
My boy swears it's the pilot
from the fair, the one who flew
kids up and down the river,
let them skim the tops of trees.
I take hold of his shoulder,
squeeze till he's at attention.
That's a life flight, I tell him.
It's bound for the hospital.
He's still, rigid even, and
I fight an urge to ruffle
his hair. Westward, the chopper
carries someone who is hurt
beyond these hills, but the sound
trails behind, dies just this side
of all that oak and cedar.

Mine

    The morning after, there were
    thick oaks and walnuts, barreled
    lengths filling the field, and when

    I walked among them I thought
    of mares and colts bolting in
    the wind-swirled night, fragile legs

    snapping, bones jagged as the
    broken ends of storm-lashed limbs.
    But we were blessed, nine horses

    out of nine, all huddled like
    cattle in the far corner
    of the pasture. *They are fine,*

    Julie said, *frightened but fine.*
    I thought so too until I
    read their eyes, and through theirs, mine.

Restoration

>Property of ancestors
>I never knew, passed to me
>as eldest grandchild, it sat
>
>on a closet shelf until
>an uncle who knew fiddles
>carried it home to his shop,
>
>coaxed music from deadened strings.
>I envisioned him bowing
>clouds of dust into the air,
>
>strands of horsehair screeching like
>devils of hell, but when he
>uncased the fiddle and pinched
>
>its strings between fingers that
>could have been my grandfather's,
>I felt old rhythms frolic
>
>in my blood, heard jig-bow's hard
>stomp and manic pace, knew then
>Ozark soil would hold me too.

White-tail

    At night they mat orchard grass
    to flat ovals, browse garden
    rows by dawn, till the back door

    claps behind me and springing
    haunches launch them beyond tilled
    soil toward viney green walls of

    understory—fleet crashing
    of hoof, leaf, limb—then the long
    day's silence of their going.

Axe, Fire, Mule

Last summer the banks of my
pond bore hoof scars where cattle
lumbered down to stand hock-deep
in drought dregs and drink. Now crops

rot beneath constant cloudspill
while I watch brown water wash
across land my grandfather
cleared with axe, fire, mule. Heart raw,

I work hours in soaked boots, ask
how water can be mock of
God one day, print of his hand
the next. Maybe old Noah

knew, but nothing's sure for me
except Julie and the kids
need all that's left of us here.
We'll stay, start over—rain, shine.

Rose of Sharon

Rose of Sharon

Mowing in midday heat, I veer too close,
clip the trunk of a blooming bush whose roots
wrap rocks chipped from mountains worn down

to ridges. July is the dry season, drought
never more than two weeks out in Ozark lore.
Stooping, I check the marred bark of the

Rose of Sharon, note purple petals drooping
like weary single mothers whose names
dot my class rolls. Months ago I taught

The Grapes of Wrath, stressed some Ozarkers
had been Okies too, swallowing gall along
the length of the mother road until they spilled

spent selves into the false dream of the
San Joaquin. Hearing this heritage, even
the hard cases leaned forward, hands leaving

pockets to squeeze desk corners, sometimes
wave for attention. What they told me
they told each other, that the look which passed

between Rose of Sharon and her mother
at the end of the book was a woman's blessing
on the best thing her daughter would ever do.

Remembering, I drip sweat to parched earth
and finger broken bark, note the gashed shaft,
the subtle listing from center that is unlikely

to cure itself with time. Lacking a gardener's
gift for care, tempted by the cooling balm
of central air, I follow the graveled path

to the shed, search out twine and stake,
heft an old hammer and return, determined
to discover what good, if any, my hand might do.

Downsized

I knew him first as the tough
talker on the junior high
bus, one seat behind me and
giddy that he'd knocked Dan Sims

to the sidewalk, his prize a
tooth-deep gash reddening his
knuckles, fresh wound he cherished
like gold. No prize shines for him

now as he glowers from the
back of my classroom, sullen
machinist gone paunchy with
beer, each essay a curse he

hurls at *greedy bosses* or
lazy Mexicans whose checks
should be his. The anger sparks
hotter with every paper

I return, margins marred by
red ink—bitter evidence
I can offer only words
to lift him from the sidewalk.

English as a Second Language

First—she tells me—
she writes every sentence
in her own language,

to know she has said
what she means to say,
then worries it out again,

word for word, in mine—
this tongue she hears
all day from a hundred

monolingual mouths—
but so much flows by
so fast she feels like

Lucy stuffing bonbons,[3]
and fears the laugh track
plays just to mock her.

---

[3] Lucille Ball: American actress and comedian who starred in the classic situation comedy *I Love Lucy*. The famous chocolate scene from that program is an iconic part of television history.

Speech Lessons

English only insist the
barber shop boys, their voices
booming as John's scissors lisp,
raspy faint, about my ears
like a whispering conscience.
Mute, sullen in my chair, I
remember this morning's class
when one student stood against
the rest, damning warrantless
wiretaps while classmates shook heads,
grinned, traded behind her back
common jokes about Juarez
English. Fumbling, I hinted
how their listening had been
tainted, groomed to greet accent
as content, messenger as
message, but their faces gave
back scowls, their lips grumblings. Now
my mouth stays sealed as grown men
laud their native tongue while they
pronounce Ozark towns—namesakes
like Bolivar, Potosi,
even Versailles—as if the
past had never been. John has
kept his chair for forty years,
scissors clipping softly while
his voice, like mine today, stays
still. I rise, tip a dollar,
and we nod, our long habit
of parting yet unbroken
by words of any language.

Sign

I mistook her eyes, read her
steady front-row gaze as sign
she wished to read Ted Kooser's
"Memory" aloud. By line's

end, when she had failed to sound
out the two syllable word
cornshucks or make letters stand
still, I knew I had run a

red light, hit someone in the
crosswalk. *I'm confused,* she said,
stopping. Grateful, I prompted
another, who read the long

poem like the whirlwind it
is. Silence followed the last
word, until I asked what the
poem described. *Tornado*

she offered from the front row,
her gaze now steady again.
I nodded, bowing to the
bravest person in the room.

Following Mr. Parks

Although I know the adjunct
by name alone, I carry
the news like an ulcer when
I enter this windowless

room, fluorescents flaring. Two
early students stare, a girl
front row center, a man—dour,
booted and blue-jeaned—planted

in a back corner. Dread dumbs
my tongue as I spread papers
across the desk, scan the roll—
names without faces. *Where is*

Mr. Parks, asks the girl, her
smile unguarded. What words I
find are bare facts, my voice flat.
He passed last night, I tell her.

A heart attack. Her eyes flit
from me to empty lectern,
to hands now clasped in her lap.
Silently she weeps. Rows back,

the man rises. Blunt boot heels
thump as he strides the aisle, takes
a chair beside the girl. His
rough hand reaches, spanning space.

Endgame

In memory she arrives without sound,
ghosting into my office while I scan
yet another essay, but as I lift
my gaze she is there, weeping, her left eye

bruised blacker than the coffee I've just poured.
This time I'm leaving him, she rasps. *I won't
be in class anymore.* Nodding, I push
papers aside, hope that something worthy

sneaks past my lips, but before one word comes
she turns, pads down the hall. I wait too long
to rise, am late getting to the exit
and can spot her nowhere on the grounds when

I burst outside, staring at the now strange
faces of students, a few of whom call
me by name. Wind moves among maple leaves
as I walk this softly autumned campus,

my bruised pupil impossible to find.
At the street corner I stop short, note a
curled condom on the curb, marvel at how
chancy the endgames of human embrace.

Revision

I remember him lingering after
class, watched as he eyed the door to make sure
we were alone. He was a broad man, thick

through the chest and torso, prison tattoos
encircling each arm until skin and ink
disappeared beneath the grimy, faded

sleeves of his service station uniform.
As he started toward the desk I made a
mental note of his grades, pondered whether

anything I'd said during class might have
given offense. Dread of argument left
my mind when he asked about misspellings,

run-ons, best ways to end a paragraph.
Then, as the clock ticked toward ten and the
maintenance man poked his head into the

room a third time, my student finally
asked the real question, *How can somebody
like me find work that's clean?* I thought he meant

employment that would keep him out of jail,
but he pointed to my right hand, held up
his own to show even the cracks stained by

grease. *I'm sick to my soul of dirt,* he said,
then let the hand drop like a useless limb.
Briefly I pictured that hand in childhood,

the skin still soft, without callous or stain.
He had marred the surface, wished to disown
his old dirt. Searching for words, I fell back

on the night's lesson, professed faith that first
drafts are always flawed, beauty only brought
into view through relentless revision.

At Shiloh

There is no blood at Bloody Pond,
only the historian's voice
at noon conjuring a sunset
vision: tattered troops crawl to pond's
edge, tortured by wound-induced thirst
while cannon boom above, tinder
aflame in encircling woods. Thrilled
by the red-drenched vision, we munch
sandwiches, stare at the garish
pond of 1862 till
a fish flops, stopping the scholar
mid-sentence. Chuckling ourselves toward
silence while pond ripples fade, we
shuffle clumsy feet, moving away.

Soldier Home

    Her essay about how she got her wound
would do Papa Hemingway proud, the lines
so close to the vest you'd think her piece might
be about another, louder soldier

home from Iraq, one she overheard and
judged his stark story true enough it should
be shared, the details about heat, boredom,
thirst all shining with authenticity,

until she comes to the part about the
bullets ripping her own shoulder, how they
knocked her backward and she began to crawl
through the dirt and dust of alien land,

her own moaning vibrating in her ears
like a foreign tongue in which she could not
call the word mother. Upon reading that,
you lower the essay to your desk, pass

your hand across the surface as if to
smooth a phantom wrinkle, and wonder what
words you, or even Papa, might compose
to make fit welcome for a soldier home.

Old Order

I've just jilted Laura Ingalls Wilder
again, her Mansfield home in my rearview
before I remember, doing eighty,
to stop at Rocky Ridge, see where she penned
her prairie tales. A few miles more and I
roll into Webster County, double-take
though I've seen this sight before: plain horse and
buggy clipping hard along the shoulder,
straight-backed man and woman in black, their stares
locked on the far hilltop as if the world
were a tunnel, no need to glance right or
left. I speed past, trailing a buffeting
wind in my wake, though not even the horse
flinches. Like Laura and Almanzo, the
couple receding in my rearview seem
members of an old order, lives tracing
a stark, remnant path through the turning world.

Will and Testament

Cicero Jack, Farmer, Rues the Ruin of an Ozark River

They might as well track clay mud
on my great-aunt's Persian rug,
beer-swilling week-enders down
from Springfield or St. Louis,
hell-bent to float a clear stream
where they swear litter laws don't
apply and local accents
prove inbreeding. Yesterday
I watched one fool stand and whiz
till he flipped his hooting friends
face first into the current,
their aluminum canoe
upended while they waded,
wobbling and cursing, toward the
near bank. *Watch for moccasins*
I called to one drunk sloshing
beneath limbs, but he stared back
as if I'd sprouted a horn
from my forehead. That's when I
left them to serpents as their
natural kin. But later,
my truck stalled in the middle
of Brixey Bridge, I spotted
their stone-stoved canoe adrift
in swift water. My heart kicked
like the time I came upon
a thrown rider down Devil's
Backbone; and old as I am
I shinnied that bank praying
my body would muster strength
to rescue what I could. The
canoe cradled only shoes,
an Orvis cap, and empties
of Coors and Busch. Knee-deep or
better, river rock rolling

beneath my feet, I wrestled
the whole mess to dry ground, scanned
that noon-bright surface until
hyena giggles carried
over the water to tell
me they'd survived, would return
to weekday suits, paisley ties.

Cicero Jack Considers the Cougar's Return

> *When we came to this valley*
> *there were a good many panthers in the mountains.*
> —Theodore Pease Russell

They took the last cat the year I was born,
some lone survivor stalking boggy backwaters
of the bootheel. I imagine him crouched

in the fork of trunk and limb, a tawny ball
growling down on the dogs before the bullet
battered his brain, darkening all. Somewhere

a photo shows his carcass stretched at the feet
of stern-faced hunters, their rifles lined like
fence posts. A decade later, hill men still told

old tales learned from grandfathers, and I grew
taller listening to firelight voices lift in pitch
when panther lore storied the night. If you

hear one past dark, they'd say, you'll think
some woman's screaming for life, or they'd
picture pioneers down on the White or Buffalo,

men who would legend themselves hunting
yellowed eyes by torchlight, or sometimes
tangling hand and knife before stumbling away

half alive, their gazes fixed to distant ridges.
I've passed more than eighty years on such tales,
no fondness for rumors of cougars that

managed to ghost Ozark creek bottoms
or cragged overlooks without leaving a track,
a scrape, a pile of their own scat. But now

comes this year of proof—young males shot
by ranchers or caught on film by trail cameras,
one scarcely half a mile away.

Conservation agents say they're moving
out of Nebraska, maybe South Dakota,
wanderers scouting new territory, inspiring

paranoia when backyard pets turn up dead.
I know the difference between a coyote's kill
and something more, but still ponder why

I've taken to my porch these last few nights,
listening for something other than the bark
of dogs or bawl of cattle. I've caught

the swooped flush of owl's wings, awakened—
startled—to the faint, near-dawn chittering
of smaller things, but mostly I hear the

rattle-hiss of my own night breath, systole,
diastole, the heart's stubborn memory:
they took the last cat the year I was born.

Cicero Jack Contemplates Heart-Stays People

My daughters worry with words, more so than
sons who fence hearts, won't transgress boundaries
without invitation. Both daughters fled

these hills to wed city men, but now fret
raw nerves over me alone on this ridge
where kin have dwelt for three generations.

I spoke an hour just yesterday, the phone
numbing my good ear while I sought fit words
to tell my eldest about the Osage

and their little band that stayed, wouldn't part
from sacred soil like the rest but planted
themselves on the spot of ground they loved, till

kin began to call them Heart-Stays, meaning
mock or praise I do not know. Often my
daughters' tones go soft, seem full of plea, but

behind my back I fear they use words like
stubborn or mule, frantic I quit ridges
steep enough to tilt tractors, or sell the

roan mare who kicks hind heels like a show bronc
that won't be broken. I surely wish those
girls could shut a door on dread-fears, let their

eyes remember pastures they've known since birth.
They learned to walk stony ground. Their children,
like the Osage, were meant to stride this land.

Cicero Jack Ponders Relics of the Osage

I've hunted arrowheads deep
in Ozark woods, rummaged lengths
of dry creek beds to swell my
cache of hand-chipped stone, layer
the bottom drawer of the
parlor desk with a litter
of flaked flint and chert. But now,
as a killing drought lowers
water levels, turns the rich
soils of lakes and streams, I read
of scoundrels digging bones, thieves
harvesting relics of the
long dead Osage, and I must
count myself kin to both tribes.
I have plundered precious things,
and beyond my final breath
I and mine will be plundered,
soil of my progeny turned
like the loam beneath the lake.

Cicero Jack and Snake at Sunset

In the country you grow up
knowing the ground must be watched,
safe only in winter when

cold has seeped so deep that soil
and rock feel like one, till earth
turns toward fecund days thick

with weed and budded leaf, the
jutted stone crowned by a brown
coil you cede space if not fear.

Stooping, you fill one palm with
the harsh heft of stone, listen
to the clatter-crack of rock

on rock and curse, thrilled when the
copperhead streams rugged ground
toward sunset woods. After

deep breath you bend again, fill
both palms and follow, tracing
an invisible path now

gilded by lowering sun
until you reach woods' edge, where
you stare beneath crosshatch of

limb gloom and wonder how far
your need to know might lead. Stones
still pronged in hand, you heave one,

another, the percussions
thudding as you study ground
shadow-patterned by leaves long

autumned. A lack of motion
warns you back. You freeze, sentried
in the reddening swath of

the evening, a lifting breeze
like Eve at your side, silence
all the guide you want or need.

Cicero Jack Remembers Tom Cochran's Boy

Rustle is a quiet word.
It mimics the careless brush
of pant leg against sage, or
the lisp of paper money
as one man fingers bills drawn
from another's wallet, but
in practice the act fills nights
with the bawl of cattle and groan
of gears, loud proof men will
risk liberty and limb to
glom gain from another's toil.
Twenty years ago I cut
truck lights and came upon young
rustlers working hard to haul
my best bull out of state. I
leveled a rifle before
freezing them in a flashlight's
beam, heard the elder curse while
the younger lifted hands like
a villain from a vintage
Western. He meant to look fierce,
but wore a profile I knew:
Aren't you Tom Cochran's boy? The
flinch told me delivery
to a hard-jawed daddy would
be sentence enough, but those
days meanness held me in hawk's
grip. I stood both thieves in my
truck bed, lashed hands to the rack,
and drove across the county
for the pleasure of marching
frightened boys up jailhouse steps.
The younger one shivered when
he sighted cells, as I flinched
this morning when I opened
the paper to his aged face
pictured above a single

column obituary—
no mention of the nine mile
chase or deputy's bullet,
only a list of good deeds
done in intervals between
crimes and incarcerations.

The Late Love Song of Cicero Jack

How could I forget Ross Pentecost
is a widower now, wife gone since
summer? Today I failed to place him
as he shuffled down the coffee aisle,

stooped farmer come to town in Sunday
boots and straw Stetson, mirror image
I avoid. When he spoke—thin-voiced, face
a wrecked ship—my tongue grew stone-heavy.

I couldn't think past her absence, how
without her he looked cleaved in two, a
torso shorn of arms, legs. I nodded
before slinking away like a thief,

shame no comfortable coat to wear.
Shedding its weight has led me to this
shaded ground, Ann's resting place we chose
together. For half my life I passed

each night reclined at her side, her flesh
woman-warm beneath my hands. She gave
me sons, daughters, a bright span of days
full enough I never thought to voice

the word *empty*, nor plumb its meaning.
Pentecost's eyes told me he has searched
that void, strained to spot a floor beneath
its dark depths—a vigil I have been

too cowardly to keep. Ann deserved
a braver man, one better practiced
in tallying the countless penny
kindnesses on which spirit is spent.

The Will and Testament of Cicero Jack

> *... within me the tree*
> *of bones is giving way ...*
> —R. T. Smith

From this porch I can scan the same ridges
my father did, be proud I've kept them clear
of crowded subdivisions that bear such

names as Quail's Nest or Fox Run, where people
pass lives I cannot understand, their land
diced down to thin fractions of a single

acre, their sunsets blocked by neighbors' roofs.
Two weeks ago in Tulsa I stood at
the window of a great-grandson's room, saw

twenty feet of backyard and wondered where
he'd find space to run, or whether being
boxed in on every side by tract houses

of identical brick would still-birth all
his bodily ambition. I admit
I'm an old man with hardened ways, stubborn

beyond sense in the eyes of kin, but if
I could pronounce my clear will to the world
and have it heard, I'd defend that boy's right

to pace his own days, not have his living
sped up just to double the jingle in
someone else's pocket. That Tulsa tract

betokens business that's beyond my span
of years, hints at the windfall hopes of heirs
who wish this farm converted to bass boats

and bank accounts. One day their wants are sure
to win, but not while I breathe. A man can
live no testimony other than his

own, the inside of his story the one
true possession he can never bequeath,
the tale he must clasp bone-close in the grave.

C. D. Albin

    C. D. Albin was born and reared in West Plains, Missouri, and earned a Doctor of Arts in English from the University of Mississippi. He has taught for many years at Missouri State University—West Plains, where he founded and edits *Elder Mountain: A Journal of Ozarks Studies.* In 2017 his collection of short stories, *Hard Toward Home*, won the Missouri Author Award for Fiction from the Missouri Library Association. His stories, poems, and reviews have appeared in numerous periodicals, including *American Book Review*, *Arkansas Review*, *The Cape Rock*, *The Georgia Review*, *Harvard Review*, and *Natural Bridge*.

    Photographs are done by the author's sister, Kelli Albin, who earned her commercial art degree from Oral Roberts University, and her master's degree plus certifications in art and reading from Missouri State University. She is currently teaching photography at MSU-West Plains, and art K-12 at Dora School in Dora, MO.

www.ingramcontent.com/pod-product-compliance
Lightning Source LLC
Chambersburg PA
CBHW071537080526
44588CB00011B/1702